Miss Poss
A 40-Day A with J

Adapted from Walk with Jesus: A 40-Day Journey to the Cross and Beyond

Who Is Jesus?

Most everyone agrees that Jesus was a real man. Many agree that He was killed for His teachings. But most people do not agree about who He really was—and is—or what He really taught.

So what *is* the truth about Jesus? For the next 40 days, you can be the detective on the case, using the files in this book to find out who Jesus really is. Watch and listen as He teaches, as He helps His friends, and as He faces His enemies. Here you'll find the clues, the facts, and the inside information you need to uncover the truth about Jesus and His teachings.

Here's your first clue: Pay special attention to the *Words for the Wise*, and use your Bible to check out the Scriptures noted in each file. There you'll find even more facts and clues to who Jesus really is.

Now let's get started on the case. Solving it will be the adventure of a lifetime—an adventure that will bring you closer to Jesus. It's a . . .

. . . Mission Possible!

The Lazarus Files

FROM JOHN 11:1–57; MARK 11:15–18

The Inside Scoop on the Pharisees and Sadducees

Jesus had been to Jerusalem many times, and He often went to the Temple to teach. But what He said made the religious leaders—the Pharisees and the Sadducees (the priests)—very angry. They felt foolish around Jesus because He challenged their made-up laws; and He showed how they cheated God's worshipers in the Temple. The priests and the Pharisees hated Jesus! So they began to work together—to try to trap Him.

But when Jesus helped a friend in a most amazing way, the priests and the Pharisees decided that Jesus must die!

The **Pharisees** were Jewish leaders who insisted that God's law be followed exactly. The problem? They often added their own laws to God's law!*

Clue

Jerusalem was the Holy City of the Jewish people, where the Temple was located.**

Fact

The Lazarus File

Lazarus was Jesus' friend and follower. He lived in the town of Bethany. When Lazarus became very sick, his sisters Mary and Martha sent for Jesus. But by the time Jesus arrived, Lazarus had already been dead for four days. Jesus wept when He saw how sad His friends were.

Jesus was led to the tomb, which was a cave with a large stone covering the entrance. Jesus said, "Move the stone away." Then He cried out loudly, "Lazarus, come out!" And the dead man came out! He was alive!

Many people saw what Jesus did that day, and many believed in Him. But some went and told the Pharisees what He had done.

"If we let Him continue doing these miracles," they said, "everyone will believe in Him." So that day . . .

. . . they began planning to kill Jesus.

inside information

Usually the Pharisees and the Sadducees hated each other, but they hated Jesus even more!

The Sadducees were the Jewish leaders who controlled the Temple. They were the high priests.*

Clue

The King Comes to Jerusalem

FROM MATTHEW 21:1–11

The Triumphal Entry

It was almost time for the Jewish Passover Feast in Jerusalem, and Jesus came to the city for the feast. He rode into Jerusalem like a king—not like an earthly king with rich robes and jewels. No! Jesus rode on the humble colt of a donkey.

The donkey was a message to the priests and the Pharisees. Long ago the prophet Zechariah had said: "Tell the people of Jerusalem,

> 'Your king is coming to you . . .
> He is gentle and riding on a donkey.'"
> —Zechariah 9:9

Jesus was telling the priests and the Pharisees that He was the true King of Israel. And they were furious! But they could not arrest Jesus there, because thousands of His followers had gathered to welcome Him. The followers cut branches from the trees and took off their own coats to lay on the road before Him. Everyone was shouting "*Hosanna!*" Then Jesus went into Jerusalem . . .

. . . and the whole world was about to change forever!

 Fact Hosanna means "Save us now!"*

4

Clue

The priests and Pharisees wanted to trap Jesus, but Jesus trapped them instead!

A Trap for the Pharisees!

FROM MATTHEW 21:33–46

Jesus went to the Temple and told this parable:

The Vineyard

Jesus said, "There was a man who owned a vineyard. He leased the vineyard to some farmers and went away on a trip. When it was time for the grapes to be picked, the man sent his servants to get his share of the grapes. But the farmers killed the servants. The man sent more servants, but they were killed too. So the man sent his son to the farmers. But the farmers said, 'If we kill the owner's son, then the vineyard will be ours!' So they grabbed the son and killed him."

Jesus asked, "What will the vineyard owner do to the farmers when he comes?"

The priests and Pharisees said, "He will kill those evil men! Then he will lease the vineyard to other farmers."

Jesus said, "God's kingdom will be taken from you and given to those who do what God wants."

The priests and the Pharisees knew Jesus was talking about them. They wanted to arrest Jesus on the spot, but they were still afraid of the people.

They would have to wait just a little longer.

Fact

A **parable** is a story that teaches a lesson.*

5

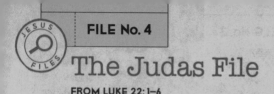
The Judas File

FROM LUKE 22:1–6

It was almost time for the Passover Feast. The priests and Pharisees had been waiting for a chance to arrest Jesus. They had to be careful, because Jesus had so many followers. Then one day, they got their chance. One of Jesus' own apostles came to see them!

Judas Iscariot was one of Jesus' 12 apostles. But Satan entered Judas, and he went to the priests and some of the soldiers who guarded the Temple. He offered them a way to arrest Jesus quietly. They were very pleased, and they promised to pay Judas for betraying Jesus. Then Judas began to watch and wait . . .

. . . he waited for a chance to betray Jesus.

✓Fact

The **Passover Feast** was celebrated each year by the Jewish people to help them remember how God had rescued them from slavery in Egypt.*

The Twelve Apostles
(MARK 3:16–19)

ERTEP _____

NRWEDA _____

MSEAJ _____

HOJN _____

LIHIPP _____

OMOLWEHATRB _____

TATHWEM _____

MTASOH _____

AESJM ONS FO PHLAAUSE _____

_____

DESAHDUTA _____

NOIMS _____

DAJUS _____

My Notes on the Case

_____

_____

_____

_____

_____

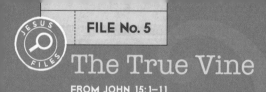

The True Vine

FROM JOHN 15:1–11

Jesus was running out of time, but there was still so much to teach His disciples. So He told them another parable:

The True Vine

Jesus said, "I am the true vine; my Father is the gardener. If a person remains in me and I remain in him, then he produces much fruit. But without me he can do nothing. Remain in me and follow my teachings" (John 15:1, 5, 7).

Jesus meant that if His disciples would love and obey Him, then their lives would be very productive—they would become more and more like Jesus.

It is the same for you. If you remain in Jesus—by loving and obeying Him—then . . .

. . . you will honor God with your life.

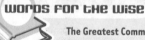

WORDS FOR THE WISE

The Greatest Command is: "Love the Lord your God with all your heart, soul and mind" (Matthew 22:37).

The Second Greatest Command is: "Love your neighbor as you love yourself" (Matthew 22:39).

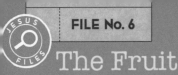

FILE No. 6

The Fruit

FROM JOHN 15:7–8

Jesus said you should produce fruit in your life to show that you are His follower. What kind of fruit did He mean?

Well, Jesus didn't say exactly, but He wasn't talking about apples or oranges or kiwis! The fruit that Jesus talked about could be helping someone else to believe in Him. Or it could be the fruit of the Spirit talked about in Galatians 5:22–23. Or it could simply be doing the right thing.

God has blessed each of you with your own special talents and gifts, so each of you may produce a different kind of fruit. Just remember these two things: Love God. Love your neighbor.

And you will be overflowing with fruit!

words for the wise

> But the Spirit gives love, joy, peace, patience, kindness, goodness, faithfulness, gentleness, self-control (Galatians 5:22–23).

See if you can unscramble all nine of the fruits of the Spirit.

FELS-TLROONC

LTNEGESNSE

THAIFFLUESSN

OODGSENS

IDESKNINS

TECPIENA

VOEL   YJO   AEECP

9

A Different Kind of King

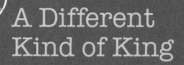

The Jews at the time of Jesus wanted a king. They wanted an earthly king who would:

* defeat their Roman conquerors (Luke 24:20–21).
* feed the people, as Jesus had done when He miraculously fed 5000 men and their families with the lunch of one boy (John 6:1–15).
* establish a great Jewish nation, as King David had done (John 6:15).

But God had a plan for a different sort of king. God wanted a King who would:

* defeat Satan (Luke 10:17–20; John 12:31).
* feed the souls of all people with forgiveness and freedom from sin and death (John 3:16–18).
* establish a heavenly kingdom that would reign for all eternity (John 18:36).

That was God's plan for Jesus . . .

. . . and Jesus knew that His death on the cross was also God's plan.

Decipher the secret clues below for a key to who Jesus really is.

For **ODG** loved the **RLDOW** so **HUMC** that he **VEAG** his only **ONS**. **ODG** gave his **ONS** so that **ERHOWEV LEISVEEB** in **IMH** may not be **TSOL**, but have **NRETALE** life (John 3:16).

WORDS FOR THE WISE

"My kingdom does not belong to this world. If it belonged to this world, my servants would fight so that I would not be given over to the Jews. But my kingdom is from another place (John 18:36)."

Fact

The **Roman Empire** had captured the Jewish lands—including Jerusalem—about 60 years before Jesus' birth.**

My Notes on the Case

_____

_____

_____

_____

The Battle

FROM MATTHEW 20:17–19; MARK 10:32–34; LUKE 18:31–33

The last few days before Jesus' crucifixion were a battle—not a battle with swords and spears, but a battle of good versus evil. A battle of truth and lies.

Jesus asked the people to believe in Him and obey His commands: Love God, and love your neighbor (Matthew 22:37–39).

It was a new way of thinking. A new covenant with God. Put what is best for others before what you want.

But the priests and the Pharisees—and especially Satan—did not want a new way of thinking. They wanted to keep doing things the old way. The Pharisees wanted to control the people with their made-up rules.

You must fight the same battle today. You have a choice. You can either choose to love and obey Jesus. Or you can follow the ways of this world.

Which do you choose?

WORDS FOR THE WISE

Our fight is not against people on earth. We are fighting against the rulers and authorities and the powers of this world's darkness. We are fighting against the spiritual powers of evil in the heavenly world (Ephesians 6:12).

The Blind Leaders

FROM MATTHEW 23:23–24, 26

The Pharisees were—well—they were show-offs. They wanted everyone to see how holy they were—how they followed God's law exactly. To prove how holy they were, they even added their own made-up laws to God's law. But they forgot why God gave the people His law. And they didn't like it when Jesus reminded them!

> Jesus said to them, "How terrible for you, teachers of the law and Pharisees! You are hypocrites! You give to God one-tenth of everything you earn . . . But you don't obey the really important teachings of the law—being fair, showing mercy, and being loyal. These are the things you should do, as well as those other things. You guide the people, but you are blind!" (Matthew 23:23–24).

To **tithe** was to give a tenth of one's income or property as an offering to God.*

Jesus also told His followers: "Stay away from the Pharisees. They are blind leaders. And if a blind man leads another blind man . . .

The Pharisees controlled the people by making them follow their made-up laws.

Clue

. . . then both men will fall into a ditch" (Matthew 15:14).

13

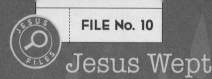

FILE No. 10

Jesus Wept
FROM LUKE 19:41–44

As Jesus entered Jerusalem for the last time, His followers shouted His praises. But Jesus wept.

> Jesus said to Jerusalem, "I wish you knew today what would bring you peace! But you can't know it. . . . A time is coming when your enemies will build a wall around you . . . They will destroy you and all your people. Not one stone of your buildings will be left on another. All this will happen because you did not know the time when God came to save you" (Luke 19:42–44).

God had sent Jesus to save the people of Jerusalem. But Jesus already knew that Jerusalem would reject Him—would crucify Him—and because of that, in A.D. 70 . . .

. . . the city would be completely destroyed!

 Fact

Jerusalem was completely destroyed by the Roman army in A.D. 70.

Jerusalem had been the Holy City of the Israelites since the time of King David. It was the Israelites' greatest city.**

14

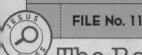

The Robbers' Hideout

FROM MATTHEW 21:12–13

> **Clue**
>
> The priests turned God's Temple into a money machine for themselves. It was even know as the Annas Bazaar.

The Scoop on the Robbers

People brought animals to the Temple to sacrifice to God. The priests checked each animal to make sure it was perfect for God. But some priests would say the animal was no good and make the people buy another one from the Temple merchants. Those animals cost too much money! The merchants would then share the money with the priests. That was cheating!

The people also had to pay a Temple tax with a special Temple coin. The moneychangers would cheat the people when they traded their coins for the Temple coins. They were robbing God's worshipers—and the priests were helping them!

Cleaning Out the Temple

When Jesus came to Jerusalem, He went to the Temple. He threw out all the people who were buying and selling there. He turned over the moneychangers' tables. Then He said,

> "It is written in the Scriptures, 'My Temple will be a house where people will pray.' But you are changing God's house into a 'hideout for robbers'" (Matthew 21:13).

The priests hated Jesus more than ever!

15

The Truth about Speaking the Truth

When you decide to stand up for Jesus, to do what is right, and to tell the truth—it won't always be easy. But keep these four things in mind:

1. Know Your Mission.

Remember who you are—*a child of God*—and what you believe in—*the teachings of Jesus*. Then . . .

> *"Go and make followers of all people in the world. Baptize them in the name of the Father and the Son and the Holy Spirit. Teach them to obey everything that I have told you" (Matthew 28:19–20).*

2. Speak Up!

It is important to speak up—when you see someone who needs to hear about Jesus or when you see something that is wrong. It can be tough when you are young, but remember that the Bible says:

"You are young, but do not let anyone treat you as if you were not important. Be an example to show the believers how they should live" (1 Timothy 4:12).

3. It's Risky, But It's Worth It.

It can be risky to speak up. Others might not like it—they may make fun of you or get angry. You may lose a friend or have a hard time at school. But remember Jesus said:

"You can be sure that I will be with you always" (Matthew 28:20).

4. There Are No Guarantees.

When you speak up for Jesus, there are no guarantees about what will happen—at least not in this world. Satan is the ruler of this world, and he can make things difficult here. But Jesus said:

"Those who are treated badly for doing good are happy. The kingdom of heaven belongs to them" (Matthew 5:10).

Who Washed the Feet?

FROM JOHN 13:1–18

Jesus and His followers had gathered for the Passover Feast. During the meal Jesus stood up and wrapped a towel around His waist. Then He took a bowl of water and began to wash His followers' feet.

But when it was Peter's turn, he said, "No! You can't wash my feet!"

Jesus said, "If I don't wash your feet, then you are not one of my followers."

Peter said, "Wash my hands and my head also!"

But Jesus said, "If a person has had a bath, he only needs to wash his feet."

After Jesus had finished washing His followers' feet, He said, "If I, as your Lord and Teacher, can wash your feet, then you also should wash each other's feet.

"I did this as an example for you" (John 13:15).

Washing the feet was usually the job of the lowest servant. No one wanted to wash feet!

Clue

inside information

Jesus washed Judas' feet.

Jesus Prays in the Garden

FROM MATTHEW 26:36–46

That night, after the meal, Jesus went with His followers to a garden called Gethsemane. Jesus was very sad and troubled. He said to Peter and the two sons of Zebedee, "My heart is full of sorrow. Stay here and watch with me."

Then Jesus walked a short distance away from them and prayed,

> "My Father, if it is possible, do not give me this cup of suffering. But do what you want, not what I want" (Matthew 26:39).

When Jesus returned to His followers, He saw that they had fallen asleep. Jesus woke them and said, "Stay awake and pray for strength against temptation" (Matthew 26:41).

Twice more Jesus went to pray, and twice more Jesus returned to find His disciples sleeping. Then Jesus said, "Wake up! We must go.

"Here comes the man who has betrayed me."

inside information

To find out who the two sons of Zebedee were, unscramble these letters.

ONJH   MESJA

Betrayed!

FROM MATTHEW 26:47–50

While Jesus was still speaking to His followers in the garden, Judas came up to them.

There were many people with him, and they were carrying swords and clubs. Judas had told them he would give them a signal. "The man I greet with a kiss will be Jesus. Arrest Him."

Immediately Judas went up to Jesus, saying, "Greetings, Teacher!" and kissed Him.

"Friend, do what you came to do," Jesus replied.

Then the men with Judas grabbed Jesus and arrested Him.

inside information

Thirty pieces of silver was about four month's wages for an ordinary worker.**

Fact

Judas had agreed to betray Jesus for thirty pieces of silver (Matthew 26:15).

Clue

The men who came to arrest Jesus were probably the Temple guards, along with some Roman soldiers (John 18:3).

Arrested!

FROM MATTHEW 26:47–56; LUKE 22:49–51; JOHN 18:10–11

Judas had betrayed Jesus and had led a group of soldiers and Temple guards to Him. When they grabbed Jesus to arrest Him, Peter reached for his sword. He struck the high priest's servant and cut off his ear.

"Put away your sword," Jesus said, and He healed the servant's ear by simply touching it.

Jesus then asked the crowd, "Why have you come after me with swords and clubs as if I were a criminal? I've been in the Temple teaching every day, but you did not arrest me there."

Then Jesus' followers left Him with the crowd and ran away.

The servant's name was Malchus (John 18:10).

inside information

Jesus could have called down an army of angels to save Him, but He knew that His arrest was all part of His Father's plan (John 18:36).

21

The Plot against Jesus

FROM MATTHEW 26:47–56; LUKE 22:47–53; JOHN 18:1–11

The Questions

Why wasn't Jesus arrested in the Temple?

Why did they come after Him in the middle of the night?

Why did they need soldiers and weapons?

The Answers

Jesus was too popular to arrest in the Temple. He had too many followers. They couldn't arrest Jesus in the city because crowds of His followers surrounded Him wherever He went. And when Jesus was alone with His disciples, they simply could not find Him.

So they needed a plan. They decided to make Jesus look like a liar and a blasphemer. Then they would have Him killed on a cross.

Clue

Blaspheme means to say bad things about God, or to claim to be God.*

Judas was the key. When Judas came to the Pharisees and offered to betray Jesus, they quickly agreed to pay him thirty silver coins for a nighttime arrest of Jesus.

Of course, they all knew that arresting Jesus was wrong, or they would have done it in the daytime when everyone could see. But Jesus never wavered. He knew His Father's plan. So Jesus said to Peter, "Put your sword back. . . .

. . . "Shall I not drink of the cup the Father has given me?" (John 18:11).

Clue

To be killed on a cross was one of the most painful and shameful ways to die.

inside information

The priests and Pharisees were afraid that Jesus' followers might rebel if they arrested Him in public. And a rebellion would bring down the wrath of Rome and its armies!

FILE No. 18

The First Trial

FROM JOHN 18:12–14; 19–24

The soldiers and the Temple guards arrested Jesus. They tied Him like a criminal and led Him to Annas, the father-in-law of the high priest for that year. Annas was very powerful.

Jesus stood in front of Annas to be questioned.

✓ **Fact**

The **Sanhedrin** was the highest court for the Jews. It was also called "the council."**

Clues

When Jesus cleaned out the Temple, He angered Annas and his family of criminals. That's why Jesus was taken to Annas first, instead of the Sanhedrin or jail.

Annas was the father-in-law of Caiaphas, who was the real high priest. But Annas still controlled the Temple.

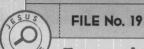

Jesus' Answer

FROM JOHN 18:19–24

Annas questioned Jesus about His followers and His teaching. Jesus answered,

> "I have spoken openly to everyone. I have always taught in synagogues and in the Temple. . . . I never said anything in secret. So why do you question me? Ask the people who heard my teaching. They know what I said." John 18:20–21

As soon as Jesus said this, one of the guards hit Him. "You shouldn't answer the high priest like that," the guard said.

Here's what Jesus said to him: "If I said something wrong, then say what was wrong. But if what I said is true, why do you hit me?" (John 18:23).

After Jesus said that, Annas sent Him to Caiaphas, the high priest.

Jesus was still tied like a criminal.

What was wrong with this trial?

* Annas was not the high priest.
* The trial took place at night, behind closed doors.
* The trial was not at the Temple.
* There were no witnesses.
* No one defended Jesus.

FILE No. 20

The Second Trial

FROM MARK 14:53–65

Even though it was very early in the morning, the members of the Jewish council—the Sanhedrin—were already secretly gathered in the high priest's palace. They tried everything to find some wrong that Jesus had done so they could kill Him. But they couldn't find one thing. Some people came and told lies about Jesus, but they couldn't even agree on their lies!

Then the high priest asked Jesus, "Are you the Christ, the Son of God?"

Jesus answered simply, "I am."

Caiaphas tore his clothes and said,

> *"We don't need any more witnesses! You all heard Him say these things against God. What do you think?"* (Mark 14:64).

The Jewish council and the priests agreed; Jesus was guilty and He should be killed. Some of them spit at Jesus, and others hit Him.

So the guards took Jesus away and beat Him.

INSIDE INFORMATION

The Sanhedrin didn't follow its own rules for a trial. They even allowed witnesses to lie.

When the Rooster Crowed

FROM LUKE 22:54–62; MARK 14: 53–54; 66–72

When Jesus was taken to the house of the high priest, Peter followed. Peter tried not to be noticed as he sat around a fire in the courtyard, near some of the soldiers. But a servant girl saw him and looked at him closely. "This man was with Jesus!" she said.

But Peter said, "I don't know Him."

A little later, another person saw Peter and said, "He's one of Jesus' followers."

"No, I'm not!" Peter said.

An hour after that, another man said, "This man is from Galilee. He was with Jesus!"

Again Peter said, "I don't know what you are talking about!"

Even while Peter was speaking, a rooster crowed. Jesus turned and looked at Peter. And Peter remembered what the Lord had said just a few hours earlier: *"Before the rooster crows tonight, you will say three times that you don't know me"* (Luke 22:61). Ashamed and brokenhearted . . .

. . . Peter ran from the courtyard and cried bitterly.

inside information

At the Passover meal, Jesus had told Peter he would deny Him three times before the rooster crowed (Matthew 26:33–35).

27

The Third Trial of Jesus

FROM LUKE 22:66

When daylight came, the older leaders of the people, the leading priests, and the teachers of the law led Jesus away to the Temple area where the Sanhedrin, their highest court, met.

At last, Jesus would face a public trial in the Temple. But it was not a fair trial, because the priests and the Pharisees had already decided . . .

. . . Jesus must die.

inside information

The public trial at the Temple was just a show for the people to keep them from rebelling.

Clue

The Sanhedrin decided that the official charge against Jesus would be treason against Rome.

FILE No. 23

I Am

FROM LUKE 22:66–71

At the Temple trial, the leading priests said to Jesus,

> *"If you are the Christ, then tell us that you are!"*
> *Jesus said to them, "If I tell you I am the Christ,*
> *you will not believe me. . . . But beginning now, the*
> *Son of Man will sit at the right hand of the powerful*
> *God."*
> *They all said, "Then are you the Son of God?"*
> *Jesus said to them, "Yes, you are right when*
> *you say that I am."*
> *They said, "Why do we need witnesses now? We*
> *ourselves heard Him say this!"* (Luke 22:67–71).

Then they led Jesus away to Pilate.

inside information

According to the Sanhedrin's own rules,
a person could not be tried, found guilty,
and sentenced to die all in the same day—
but that's just what they did to Jesus!**

Pontius Pilate was the Roman
governor over Jerusalem.**

29

JESUS FILES

Trust in the Lord

Jesus was in a terrible place, but He trusted His Father's plan for Him. God has a plan for you, too, and He wants you to trust that plan. The problem is that Satan will lie to you about God's plan—he will even tell you that God doesn't have a plan. But when you hear one of Satan's lies, fight back with one of God's truths!

The Lies of Satan	The Truths of God
You are all alone.	*"You can be sure that I will be with you always" (Matthew 28:20).*
No one loves you.	*"Yes, I am sure that nothing can separate us from the love God has for us. Not death, not life, not angels, not ruling spirits, nothing now, nothing in the future, no powers, nothing above us, nothing below us, or anything else in the whole world will ever be able to separate us from the love of God that is in Christ Jesus our Lord" (Romans 8:38–39).*
You do not matter.	*"You are the light that gives light to the world" (Matthew 5:14).*

"I know what I have planned for you," says the Lord. "I have good plans for you" (Jeremiah 29:11).

Trust the Lord with all your heart. Don't depend on your own understanding. Remember the Lord in everything you do. And he will give you success (Proverbs 3:5–6).

I was in trouble. So I called to the Lord. The Lord answered me and set me free (Psalm 118:5).

"Wear the full armor of God. Wear God's armor so that you can fight against the devil's evil tricks" (Ephesians 6:11). Put on:

» The Belt of Truth
» The Breastplate of Right Living
» The Shoes of the Good News of Peace
» The Shield of Faith
» The Helmet of God's Salvation
» The Sword of the Spirit, which is God's Word

(from Ephesians 6:14–17)

The Fourth Trial of Jesus

FROM LUKE 23:1-4; JOHN 18:28-32

The priests and the teachers of the law led Jesus to Pilate, the Roman governor. But the Jews did not go inside the Roman palace. To do so would make them unclean and keep them from eating the Passover meal. So Pilate went out to them and asked what charges they had against Jesus.

They said, "This man says we should not pay taxes to Caesar. He says He is the Christ, a king."

Pilate called Jesus to him. "Are you the king of the Jews?" he asked.

"Yes, it's true," Jesus said.

Pilate questioned Jesus some more. Then he said to the leading priests and the people gathered there . . .

"I find nothing wrong with this man" (Luke 23:4).

Clue

Pilate was the only person who could order that Jesus be put to death.**

inside information

The religious leaders knew that Rome cared only about Rome. If they wanted Pilate to execute Jesus, they would have to make Jesus look like a threat to Roman rule.

Jesus Sent to Herod

FROM LUKE 23:4–7

When Pilate said, "I find nothing wrong with this man," the priests and the Pharisees began to shout. Over and over they shouted, "But Jesus is making trouble all around Judea. He began by teaching the people in Galilee, and now He is here!"

When Pilate heard this, he asked if Jesus were from Galilee. If so, that meant Jesus was under Herod's authority. And, it just so happened that, Herod was in Jerusalem at that time . . .

. . . so Pilate sent Jesus to Herod.

inside information

Jesus was from Galilee, and Herod was ruler of Galilee. Pilate thought he had the perfect answer: Send Jesus to Herod. Let Him be Herod's problem!

Clue

Herod was in Jerusalem for the Passover Feast (Luke 23:7).

The Fifth Trial of Jesus

FROM LUKE 23:8–12

Herod had been wanting to meet Jesus. He had heard about Jesus and the many miracles He had done. Now he had a chance to see Jesus perform a miracle—in person!

Herod also had many questions for Jesus, but Jesus said nothing—not a thing! The leading priests and the Pharisees were also there, shouting at Jesus and accusing Him.

Herod and his soldiers began to make fun of Jesus. But still Jesus said nothing. Finally, they became bored and dressed Him in a kingly robe. Then . . .

. . . they sent Him back to Pilate.

inside information

Herod dressed Jesus in a kingly robe as a joke for Pilate. Herod and Pilate had always been enemies, but this "joke" over the King of the Jews made them friends.

The Sixth Trial

FROM LUKE 23:13–25

Pilate tried again to free Jesus. It was the custom at Passover to release one prisoner, and Pilate wanted it to be Jesus instead of the killer Barabbas. Talking to the people, together with the leading priests and the Pharisees, Pilate said, "I have not found this man to be guilty of what you say. I see nothing for which He should die. I will punish Him and let Him go free."

Then the people began to shout, "Kill Him! Free Barabbas!"

"Why?" Pilate asked. "What wrong has He done?"

The people continued to shout, "Kill Him on a cross!" They yelled so loudly that Pilate gave them what they wanted. He freed Barabbas . . .

. . . and he turned Jesus over to the soldiers to be killed.

Clue

Pilate would release one prisoner at the Passover Feast (John 18:39).

Fact

Barabbas was a notorious killer (Luke 23:19).

Scourging!

FROM JOHN 19:1–3

Pilate ordered soldiers to scourge, or whip, Jesus. The soldiers also took some thorny branches and twisted them into a crown. They placed it on Jesus' head and put a purple robe around Him. Then they made fun of Jesus, bowing to Him many times and saying . . .

"Hail, King of the Jews!" (John 19:3).

Scourging was called the "halfway death." The victim would be tied to a low wooden pillar and beaten with a whip.

insiDe inFormation

During a scourging, crowds of soldiers would gather around to mock the victim.

The whip used in scourging was made of leather with long straps on the end. Sharp bits of bone, pieces of metal, or broken pottery were braided into the straps.

Carrying the Cross!

FROM LUKE 23:26

The soldiers forced Jesus to carry His own cross to the place where He would be crucified. But Jesus was so weak from the scourging that He could not carry it.

A man named Simon was coming into the city from the fields. He was from the city of Cyrene. The soldiers made Simon carry the cross for Jesus. So . . .

. . . Simon of Cyrene walked behind Jesus.

inside information

A sign was hung around the prisoner's neck. It told his name and listed his crimes. The sign would then be nailed to his cross.

Fact

Prisoners were made to carry their own crosses. It was another way to torture them.

Unscramble the letters to find out the message on Jesus' sign.

IHST SI ETH NGIK FO ETH ESWJ (Luke 23:38)

37

The Facts of the Cross

Crucifixion began with the soldiers giving the victim a drink with a mild painkiller in it. But Jesus refused to drink this (Matthew 27:34).

The person's hands and feet would be nailed to the large wooden cross. The cross would then be sat upright in the ground, and the victim would be left to die.

Crucifixion was a terrible way to die. It was so terrible that the Romans only crucified slaves and criminals.**

But Jesus was not a criminal. He was not guilty of anything. He was completely innocent.

Jesus died on the cross to save the world from sin.

WORDS FOR THE WISE

Jesus said, "Father, forgive them. They don't know what they are doing" (Luke 23:34).

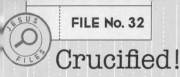

FILE No. 32

Crucified!

FROM MARK 15:22–38; LUKE 23:32–35,44–46

The soldiers led Jesus to the place called Golgotha. It was nine o-clock in the morning when Jesus was nailed to the cross. A sign was hung above Him that read: "THE KING OF THE JEWS." They also nailed two criminals to crosses, one on Jesus' left and one on His right.

The leading priests and the teachers of the law made fun of Jesus, saying, "If He is the Christ, then let Him save Himself."

At about noon the whole land became dark, and it stayed dark until three o'clock in the afternoon. Something else unusual happened too. In the Temple, the curtain was torn into two pieces. Then in a loud voice, Jesus cried out, "Father, I give you my life."

After saying this, Jesus died.

Fact

Golgotha means the Place of the Skull (Mark 15:22).

Clue

Jesus' tunic was special because it was woven in one piece. So the soldiers cast lots—or rolled dice— to see who would get it (John 19:23–24).

39

Buried!

FROM JOHN 19:38–42; LUKE 23:50–56

After Jesus died on the cross, a man named Joseph from Arimathea went to Pilate and got permission to bury Jesus. So Joseph and a man named Nicodemus took Jesus' body down from the cross. Joseph had brought with him more than 75 pounds of spices. The two men wrapped Jesus' body with the spices in pieces of linen cloth, because this was the burial custom of the time. Nearby, in a garden, there was a tomb where no one had ever been buried.

The men laid Jesus' body there.

> Joseph was a member of the Sanhedrin. He was a secret follower of Jesus because he was afraid of the religious leaders (John 19:38; Luke 23: 50–51).

Clue

Fact

> Nicodemus was also a member of the Sanhedrin, but he became a disciple of Jesus. He had once come to talk secretly to Jesus in the night (John 3:1–21).

The Tomb Is Secured

FROM MATTHEW 27:62–66

After Jesus had been buried, the leading priests and the Pharisees went to Pilate and said,

> *"Sir, we remember that while that liar was still alive he said, 'After three days I will rise from death.' So give the order for the tomb to be guarded closely till the third day. His followers might come and steal the body. Then they could tell the people that he has risen from death. That lie would be even worse than the first one."*
>
> *Pilate said, "Take some soldiers and go guard the tomb the best way you know." So they all went to the tomb and made it safe from thieves. They did this by sealing the stone in the entrance* (Matthew 27:63–66).

Then they put soldiers there to guard Jesus' tomb.

insiDe informaTion

With the tomb sealed and the soldiers standing guard, the Pharisees and the leading priests went home to observe the Sabbath and to honor God— whose Son they had just killed!

The Empty Tomb!

FROM MATTHEW 28:1–10

At dawn on the first day after the Sabbath, Mary Magdalene and another woman named Mary went to the tomb. Suddenly a strong earthquake shook the ground and an angel of the Lord came down and rolled the stone away from the entrance to the tomb. Then the angel sat on the stone, shining as bright as lightning. The soldiers guarding the tomb were so afraid that they became like dead men.

"Don't be afraid," the angel told the women. "I know you are looking for Jesus, but He is not here. Just as He said He would, He has risen from death. Go quickly and tell His followers."

When the women ran to tell Jesus' followers what had happened, they saw Jesus Himself.

The women were so happy they took hold of Jesus' feet and worshiped Him. Then Jesus asked them to tell His brothers to go on to Galilee.

"They will see me there," He said.

Clue

The women brought spices to finish the burial process. They wondered how they would move the heavy stone that covered the tomb's entrance (Mark 16:1–3).

Missing!

FROM LUKE 24:9–12;
JOHN 20:2–8

The women ran to tell the apostles everything that had happened at the tomb. The apostles thought it sounded like nonsense, and they didn't believe the women. But Peter and John got up and ran to the tomb to see for themselves.

They were both running, but John ran faster, so he reached the tomb first. When he bent down and looked in, he saw the strips of linen cloth lying there, but he did not go in.

Then came Peter. He went into the tomb and saw the strips of linen too. He also saw that the head cloth had been folded up and laid in a different place from the strips of linen.

Then John also went in.

> The linen cloth was neatly folded. It was not just thrown around—as if a grave robber had hurriedly taken the body (John 20:7).

He saw and believed.

Clue

43

Jesus' Voice

FROM JOHN 20:19–23

It was the first day of the week. Word had spread about what the women had seen, and the followers had gathered together that evening.

The doors of the room where they gathered were locked, because they were afraid of the religious leaders. Suddenly Jesus was there, standing among them and saying, "Peace be with you!" Then He showed them the wounds in His hands and His side. The followers were very happy to see Jesus again.

Jesus said, "As the Father has sent me, now I send you." Then Jesus breathed on them and said . . .

"Receive the Holy Spirit" (John 19:22).

INSIDE INFORMATION

Jesus' followers were hiding behind locked doors. They were afraid that the priests and Pharisees might come to arrest them too.

My Notes on the Case

_____

_____

_____

FILE No. 38

On the Road to Emmaus

FROM LUKE 24: 13–18

On the first day of the week, two of Jesus' followers were on their way to the town of Emmaus. They were talking about what had happened in Jerusalem during Passover. While they were talking, Jesus Himself came up to walk with them. But they did not recognize Him. "What are you talking about?" Jesus asked.

The two followers stopped to answer. They were very sad. The follower named Cleopas said . . .

> **"You must be the only one in Jerusalem who does not know what just happened there"** (Luke 24:18).

Emmaus was about 7 miles from Jerusalem (Luke 24:13).

inside information

No one knew better than Jesus what had happened in Jerusalem!

45

FILE No. 39

Believe!

FROM LUKE 24:19–31

The two men on the road to Emmaus told Jesus they were
talking about all that had happened to Jesus of Nazareth.
(They still did not know they were talking to Jesus.) "He was a
prophet from God, but the leading priests had Him killed on a
cross. We were hoping that He would free the Jews.

"It has been three days since this happened. Today some
women told us some amazing things. They said Jesus' tomb
was empty! They said they saw angels who told them Jesus
was alive! Some in our group went to the tomb, and it was
just as the women said. But they didn't see Jesus."

As they continued their walk to Emmaus, Jesus explained
everything that had been written in the Scriptures about Him,
starting with Moses and all the prophets.

When they arrived in Emmaus, the followers begged Jesus
to stay with them. Jesus stayed, and when they sat down to
eat, He gave thanks for the bread and gave it to them. Then
they were allowed to see that it was Jesus!

But as soon as they recognized Jesus, He disappeared.

My Notes on the Case

Follow Me!

FROM MATTHEW 28:16–20

Jesus told His followers to go to a mountain in Galilee. When they got there, Jesus came to them and said,

"All power in heaven and on earth is given to me. So go and make followers of all people in the world. Baptize them in the name of the Father and the Son and the Holy Spirit. Teach them to obey everything that I have told you.

"You can be sure that I will be with you always" (Matthew 28:18–20).

Jesus' mission for His followers is called **The Great Commission**.

Will You Follow Jesus?

FROM MATTHEW 28:19–20

Jesus commanded His followers to go and to teach others about Him. And He asks the same of you. God made you like no one else. You were given your own special talents. You can do things for Him that no one else can do. So . . .

. . . will you choose to follow Jesus?

References

*Youngblood, Ronald F., Bruce, F.F., and Harrison, R.K. *International Children's Bible Dictionary*. Nashville: Tommy Nelson, a division of Thomas Nelson, Inc., 2006.

**Richards, Lawrence. *International Children's Bible Field Guide*. Nashville: Tommy Nelson, a division of Thomas Nelson, Inc., 1989.